General Direc

To Cover Straps

With yarn indicated in each pattern and holding flip-flop with heel toward you, join yarn with sc around right strap near heel, holding yarn snug as you crochet, 4 sc around strap; slide sts to very end of strap (keeping top of sts on center top of strap); continue to work sc around strap until completely covered; sk toe and work sc around left strap until completely covered. Fasten off.

Follow pattern instructions to complete each design.

Embroide

French Knot

Bring yarn up. Wrap yarn around shaft of needle. Insert needle down (see Fig. 1). Pull wrapping yarn snug around needle and hold the yarn as needle is pulled through wrap; release yarn as knot tightens.

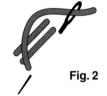

Fig. 1

Straight Stitch

Thread yarn needle with yarn. Bring needle up and down to complete stitch (see Fig. 2).

Fig. 2

Button Flower

BEGINNER

Sizes

Adult, Child

Materials

Medium (worsted) weight crochet cotton,
   small amount of light green
Note: *Our photographed trims were made with Elmore-Pisgah Peaches & Creme, baby green #54.*
For Adult: Size G/6/4mm crochet hook (for straps and design)
   or size required for gauge
For Child: Size G/6/4mm crochet hook (for straps) or size
   required for gauge; size E/4/3.50mm crochet hook
   (for design)

6 (½-inch) star-shaped buttons
Yarn needle
Sewing needle and matching thread
One pair flip-flops

Gauge

With size G hook, 6 sc = 1 inch

Instructions

Note: For adult size, use larger hook; for child size, use larger hook for straps and smaller hook for flowers.

Straps

Following General Directions above crochet over straps.

Flower (make 6)

Ch 5, join with sl st to form a ring; ch 1, in ring work [sc, 3 dc] 5 times; join in first sc.
Fasten off, leaving an 8-inch length for sewing. Weave in rem end.

Finishing

Step 1: With sewing needle and matching thread, sew one button to center of each flower.
Step 2: Referring to photo for placement and with yarn needle and long ends, sew three flowers to each strap.

Daisy

BEGINNER

Sizes
Adult, Child

Materials
Medium (worsted) weight cotton yarn,
  small amount of green, yellow and white
Note: Our photographed trims were made with Lily Sugar 'n' Cream, emerald green #62, yellow #10 and white #1.
For Adult: Size G/6/4mm crochet hook (for straps and
  design) or size required for gauge
For Child: Size G/6/4mm crochet hook (for straps) or size
  required for gauge; size E/4/3.50mm crochet hook
  (for design)
Yarn needle
One pair flip-flops

Gauge
With size G hook, 6 sc = 1 inch

Instructions
Note: For adult size, use larger hook; for child size, use larger hook for straps and smaller hook for flowers.

Straps
Following General Directions on page 1 and with green, crochet over straps.

Daisy (make 2)
Center
With yellow, ch 4; join to form a ring.

Rnd 1 (RS): Ch 1, 8 sc in ring; join in first sc. *(8 sc)*
Fasten off.

Petals
Hold center with RS facing you; join white in any sc.
Rnd 2: *Ch 5, sc in 2nd ch from hook and in next ch, sl st in next 2 chs—petal made; sl st in next sc; rep from * 6 times more; ch 5, sc in 2nd ch from hook and in next ch, sl st in next 2 chs—petal made; join in joining sl st. *(8 petals)*
Fasten off, leaving an 8-inch length for sewing. Weave in other end.

Finishing
With yarn needle and long ends, sew one daisy to center of each strap.

Forget-Me-Knots

BEGINNER

Sizes
Adult, Child

Materials
Medium (worsted) weight crochet cotton,
  small amount of white, light blue, light green and yellow
Note: Our photographed trims were made with Lily Sugar 'n' Cream, white #1, cornflower blue #83, light green #55 and yellow #10.

For Adult: Size G/6/4mm crochet hook (for straps and design) or size required for gauge

For Child: Size G/6/4mm crochet hook (for straps) or size required for gauge; size E/4/3.50mm crochet hook (for design)

Yarn needle

One pair flip-flops

Gauge

With size G hook, 6 sc = 1 inch

Instructions

Note: For adult size, use larger hook; for child size, use larger hook for straps and smaller hook for flowers.

Straps

Following General Directions on page 1 and with white, crochet over straps.

Flower (make 6)

With light blue, ch 3; join to form a ring.

Rnd 1 (RS): Ch 1, in ring work (2 hdc, ch 1, sl st)—petal made; [ch 1, in ring work (2 hdc, ch 1, sl st) 4 times—4 petals made. *(5 petals)*

Fasten off, leaving an 8-inch length for sewing. Weave in rem end.

Leaf (make 2)

With light green, ch 5; 2 hdc in 3rd ch from hook; hdc in next ch, 3 sc in next ch; working on opposite side in unused lps of beg ch, hdc in next ch, 4 hdc in next ch; join in 5th ch of beg ch-5. Fasten off, leaving an 8-inch length for sewing. Weave in rem end.

Finishing

Step 1: With yellow, make a French knot *(see General Directions on page 1)* in center of each flower.

Step 2: Referring to photo for placement and with yarn needle and long ends, sew three flowers and one leaf to each strap.

· ·

Sunflower

BEGINNER

Sizes

Adult, Child

Materials

Medium (worsted) weight crochet cotton,
  small amount of light green, brown and yellow

Note: Our photographed trims were made with Lily Sugar 'n' Cream, light green #55, warm brown #130 and yellow #10.

For Adult: Size G/6/4mm crochet hook (for straps and design) or size required for gauge

For Child: Size G/6/4mm crochet hook (for straps) or size required for gauge; size E/4/3.50mm crochet hook (for design)

Yarn needle

One pair flip-flops

Gauge

With size G hook, 6 sc = 1 inch

Instructions

Note: For adult size, use larger hook; for child size, use larger hook for straps and smaller hook for sunflowers.

Straps

Following General Directions on page 1 and with light green, crochet over straps.

Sunflower (make 2)
Center

With brown, ch 2.

Rnd 1 (RS): 12 hdc in 2nd ch from hook; join in first hdc. *(12 hdc)*

Rnd 2: Ch 1, sc in same hdc and in each rem; join in first sc. Fasten off, leaving an 8-inch length for sewing. Weave in rem end.

Petals

Hold center with RS facing you; join yellow in back lp of first sc on Rnd 2.

Rnd 1: Ch 6, working in back bumps only of chs, sl st in 3rd ch from hook, sc in next ch, hdc in next 2 chs—petal made; *sl st in back lp of next sc on Rnd 2, ch 6, sl st in 3rd ch from hook, sc in next ch, hdc in next 2 chs—petal made; rep from * 10 times more; join in front lp of first sc of Rnd 2. *(12 petals)*

Rnd 2: Ch 5, working in back bump only of chs, sl st in 3rd ch from hook, sc in next ch, hdc in next ch—petal made; *sl st in front lp only of next sc on Rnd 2 of center, ch 5, sl st in 3rd ch from hook, sc in next ch, hdc in next ch—petal made; rep from * 10 times more; join in joining sl st. *(12 petals)*
Fasten off and weave in ends.

Finishing

With yarn needle and long ends, sew one sunflower to center of each strap.

- -

Rosebud

BEGINNER

Sizes

Adult, Child

Materials

Medium (worsted) weight crochet cotton, small amount of white, light green and pink
Note: Our photographed trims were made with Lily Sugar 'n' Cream, white #1, light green #55 and rose pink #46.
For Adult: Size G/6/4mm crochet hook (for straps and design) or size required for gauge
For Child: Size G/6/4mm crochet hook (for straps) or size required for gauge; size E/4/3.50mm crochet hook (for design)
Yarn needle
One pair flip-flops

Gauge

With size G hook, 6 sc = 1 inch

Instructions

Note: For adult size, use larger hook; for child size, use larger hook for straps and smaller hook for rosebuds.

Straps

Following General Directions on page 1 and with white, crochet over straps.

Rosebud (make 2)
Stem & Leaf

With light green, ch 12 loosely; working in back bumps only, 5 hdc in 3rd ch from hook; sl st in next 3 chs, ch 3, in 3rd ch from work (hdc, ch 2, sl st); sl st in each rem ch of beg ch-12. Fasten off, leaving an 8-inch length for sewing.

Rose

Hold piece with RS facing you; working in back lps only, join pink in 2nd ch of beg 2 skipped chs of stem; ch 3 (counts as a dc), dc in same ch; 2 dc in next hdc; 3 hdc in each of next 2 hdc; 2 sc in each of next 2 hdc; 3 sc in next hdc; sl st in same st. *(17 sts)* Fasten off, leaving an 8-inch length for sewing.

Finishing

Step 1: To form rosebud, roll rosebud piece into bud shape, beg with dc in center and ending with sc on outer edge. With yarn needle and long end, tack bud in place. Rep with remaining piece.

Step 2: With yarn needle and long ends, sew one rosebud and stem to each strap.

. . . .

Black-Eyed Suzy

BEGINNER

Sizes
Adult, Child

Materials
Medium (worsted) weight crochet cotton,
  small amount of green, black and yellow
Note: Our photographed trims were made with Lily Sugar 'n' Cream, emerald #62, black #2 and yellow #10.
For Adult: Size G/6/4mm crochet hook (for straps and design) or size required for gauge
For Child: Size G/6/4mm crochet hook (for straps) or size required for gauge; size E/4/3.50mm crochet hook (for design)
Yarn needle
One pair flip-flops

Gauge
With size G hook, 6 sc = 1 inch

Instructions
Note: For adult size, use larger hook; for child size, use larger hook for straps and smaller hook for flowers.

Straps
Following General Directions on page 1 and with green, crochet over straps.

Flower (make 2)
Center
With black, ch 2.

Rnd 1 (RS): 6 hdc in 2nd ch from hook; join in first hdc. *(6 hdc)*
Rnd 2: Ch 1, hdc in each hdc; join in first hdc.
Rnd 3: Ch 1, sc in each hdc; join in first sc. Fasten off.

Petals
Hold center with RS facing you; join yellow in first sc on Rnd 3; ch 7, working in back bumps only, sl st in 2nd ch from hook and in next ch, hdc in next 2 chs, sc in next ch, sl st in next ch—petal made; *sl st in same sc on center, ch 7, sl st in 2nd ch from hook and in next ch, hdc in next 2 chs, sc in next ch, sl st in next ch—petal made; sl st in next ch on Rnd 3, ch 7, sl st in 2nd ch from hook and in next ch, hdc in next 2 chs, sc in next ch, sl st in next ch—petal made; rep from * 4 times more; sl st in same sc on Rnd 3, ch 7, sl st in 2nd ch from hook, sc in next ch, hdc in next 2 chs, sc in next ch, sl st in next ch—petal made; join in same sc on Rnd 3 as first sl st made. *(12 petals)*
Fasten off, leaving an 8-inch length for sewing. Weave in other end.

Finishing
With yarn needle and long ends, sew one flower to center of each strap.

Beaded Mum

Sizes
Adult, Child

Materials
Bulky (chunky) weight yarn, small amount pink
Note: Our photographed trims were made with Lion Brand Homespun, Queen Anne #331.
For Adult: Size G/6/4mm crochet hook (for straps and design) or size required for gauge
For Child: Size G/6/4mm crochet hook (for straps) or size required for gauge; size E/4/3.50mm crochet hook (for design)
140 (4mm) transparent bi-cone beads
Yarn needle
Sewing needle and matching thread
One pair flip-flops

Gauge
With size G hook, 5 sc = 1 inch

Instructions
Note: For adult size, use larger hook; for child size, use larger hook for straps and smaller hook for mums.

Straps
Following General Directions on page 1, crochet over straps.

Mum (make 2)
Ch 5, join to form a ring.
Rnd 1 (RS): [Ch 8, sl st in ring] 10 times. Do not join.
Rnd 2: [Ch 7, sl st between next 2 sl sts] 10 times.
Fasten off, leaving an 8-inch length for sewing. Weave in rem end.

Finishing
Step 1: With sewing needle and matching thread, sew 3 beads to each ch-7 lp on each mum.
Step 2: With yarn needle and long ends, sew one set of loops to center of each strap.

Butterfly

Sizes
Adult, Child

Materials
Medium (worsted) weight crochet cotton, small amount of green, lavender, purple, black and white
Note: Our photographed trims were made with Lily Sugar 'n' Cream, emerald green #62, soft violet #93, grape #71, black #2 and white #1.

For Adult: Size G/6/4mm crochet hook (for straps and design) or size required for gauge
For Child: Size G/6/4mm crochet hook (for straps); size E/4/3.50mm crochet hook (for design)
Yarn needle
One pair flip-flops

Gauge

With size G hook, 6 sc = 1 inch

Instructions

Note: For adult size, use larger hook; for child size, use larger hook for straps and smaller hook for butterflies.

Straps

Following General Directions on page 1 and with green, crochet over straps.

Butterfly (make 2)
Wings

With lavender, ch 6 loosely.
Rnd 1 (RS): Working in back bumps only, in 2nd ch from hook work (sl st, ch 2, hdc, ch 2, sl st)—bottom wing made; sl st in next 2 chs, in next ch work (sl st, ch 3, 2 dc, ch 3, sl st)—top wing made; in next ch work (sl st, ch 2, sl st); working on opposite side in unused lps of beg ch, in next ch work (sl st, ch 3, 2 dc, ch 3, sl st)—top wing made; sl st in next 2 chs, in next ch work (sl st, ch 2, hdc, ch 2, sl st)—bottom wing made. Do not join. Fasten off.
Rnd 2: With RS facing you, join purple in first ch-2 sp, 2 sc in same sp; hdc in next hdc, 2 sc in next ch-2 sp; ch 1, sk next sl st, sl st in next sl st, ch 1, 2 sc in next ch-3 sp; hdc in next 2 dc, in next ch-3 sp work (hdc, 2 sc); ch 1, sl st in next ch-2 sp, ch 1, in next ch-3 sp work (2 sc, hdc); hdc in next 2 dc, 2 sc in next ch-3 sp; ch 1, 2 sc in next ch-2 sp; hdc in next hdc, in next ch-2 sp work (2 sc, sl st). Do not join. Fasten off.

Body

Hold piece with RS facing you; join black beg skipped ch of beg ch-6; ch 2, sl st in back bump of 2nd ch from hook, sl st in same turning ch as first sl st, ch 8, st st in center sl st on Rnd 2 between top wings at opposite end, ch 3, sl st in same center sl st, sl st in back bump of next 8 chs, sl st in same st as beg sl st.
Fasten off, leaving an 8-inch length for sewing.

Edging
First Bottom Wing

Hold piece with RS facing you; sk first sc of Rnd 2, working in back lps only, join black in next sc; sc in next 2 sts, sl st in next st. Fasten off.
First Top Wing

Hold piece with RS facing you; sk next 2 ch-1 sp and next sc from edging on bottom wing, working in back lps only, join black in next sc; sc in next 3 sts, sl st in next sc. Fasten off.
Second Top Wing

Hold piece with RS facing you; working in back lps only, join black in 2nd sc of 2nd top wing; sc in next 3 sc, sl st in next sc. Fasten off.
Second Bottom Wing

Hold piece with RS facing you; sk next ch-1 sp of next wing, working in back lps only, join black in next sc; sc in next 2 sts, sl st in next sc. Fasten off.

Antennae

Cut one 4-inch strand of black. Fold strand in half and draw folded end through ch-3 sp at top of body. Pull ends through folded end and tighten knot. Tie knot in each end of strand and trim ends close to knots.

Finishing

Step 1: With white, make 3 French Knots *(see General Directions on page 1)* on each top wing and one French Knot on each bottom wing.
Step 2: With yarn needle and long ends, sew one butterfly to center of each strap.

Ladybug

BEGINNER

Sizes
Adult, Child

Materials
Medium (worsted) weight crochet cotton,
  small amount of white, red and black
Note: Our photographed trim was made with Lily Sugar 'n' Cream, white #1, red #95 and black #2.
For Adult: Size G/6/4mm crochet hook (for straps and design) or size required for gauge
For Child: Size G/6/4mm crochet hook (for straps) or size required for gauge; size E/4/3.50mm crochet hook (for design)
Yarn needle
One pair flip-flops

Gauge
With size G hook, 6 sc = 1 inch

> **Pattern Stitches**
> **Long single crochet** (long sc)
> Insert hook in st indicated, draw up lp to height of working row, yo and draw through 2 lps on hook.

Instructions
Note: For adult size, use larger hook; for child size, use larger hook for straps and smaller hook for ladybugs.

Straps
Following General Directions on page 1 and with white, crochet over straps.

Ladybug (make 2)
Body
Note: Body is worked in continuous rnds. Do not join; mark beg of rnds.
With red, ch 6 loosely.
Rnd 1 (RS): Sc in 2nd ch from hook and in next 3 chs, 3 sc in next ch (mark 2nd sc); working on opposite side in unused lps of beg ch, sc in next 3 chs, 2 sc in next ch. *(12 sc)*
Rnd 2: 2 sc in first sc; sc in next 3 sc, 2 sc in each of next 3 sc;

sc in next 4 sc, 2 sc in next sc. *(17 sc)*
Rnd 3: 2 sc in first sc; sc in next 6 sc, 2 sc in each of next 3 sc; sc in next 6 sc, 2 sc in next sc; join in first sc. *(22 sc)*
Fasten off, leaving an 8-inch length for sewing. Weave in rem end.

Head
Hold body with RS facing you; join black in 8th sc to left of joining sl st of Rnd 3; 3 **long sc** (see Pattern Stitch) in marked sc on Rnd 1; sl st in next sc on working rnd, 3 long sc in same marked sc; sl st in next sc on working rnd.
Fasten off and weave in ends.

Tail
Hold body with RS facing you; sk next 8 unused sc on Rnd 3 from head, join black in next sc; ch 1, sc in same sc; in next sc work (sc, ch 1, sl st).
Fasten off and weave in ends.

Finishing
Step 1: With black, make Straight Stitches *(see General Directions on page 1)* on Body to form back ridge.
Step 2: With black, make 3 French Knots *(see General Directions on page 1)* on each side of body for spots.
Step 3: For antennae, cut two 4-inch strands of black. Fold strand in half. Insert hook in 2nd long sc on head and draw folded end through. Pull ends through and tighten knot. Rep with 2nd strand in 5th long sc on head. Trim ends.
Step 4: With yarn needle and long ends, sew one ladybug to center of each strap.

Ice Cream Cone

Sizes
Adult, Child

Materials
Medium (worsted) weight crochet cotton,
   small amount of red, ecru, brown, white and pink
Note: Our photographed trims were made with Lily Sugar 'n' Cream, red #95, ecru #4, warm brown #130, white #1 and rose pink #46.
For Adult: Size G/6/4mm crochet hook (for straps and design) or size required for gauge
For Child: Size G/6/4mm crochet hook (for straps) or size required for gauge; size E/4/3.50mm crochet hook (for design)
Yarn needle
One pair flip-flops

Gauge
With size G hook, 6 sc = 1 inch

Instructions
Note: For adult size, use larger hook; for child size, use larger hook for straps and smaller hook for ice cream cones.

Straps
Following General Directions on page 1 and with red, crochet over straps.

Ice Cream Cone (make 2)
Cone
With ecru, ch 2.
Row 1 (WS): 2 sc in 2nd ch from hook. Turn. *(2 sc)*
Row 2 (RS): Ch 1, 2 sc in first sc; sc in next sc. Turn. *(3 sc)*
Row 3: Ch 1, 2 sc in first sc; sc in next 2 sc. Turn. *(4 sc)*
Row 4: Ch 1, 2 sc in first sc; sc in next 3 sc. Turn. *(5 sc)*
Do not fasten off.

Edging
Working along edge of cone in end of rows, sl st in each row to beg ch; in unused lp of beg ch work (sl st, ch 1, sl st); working along next edge, sl st in each row.

Fasten off, leaving an 8-inch length for sewing. Weave in rem end.

Ice Cream
Hold piece with RS facing you; join pink in **back lp** only of first sc of Row 4 of cone.
Row 1 (RS): Ch 1, working in back lps only, 2 hdc in same st; hdc in next 3 sc, 2 hdc in next sc; turn. *(7 hdc)*
Row 2: Ch 2, working in back lps only, sl st in first 2 hdc, [ch 2, sl st in next 2 sts] twice; ch 1, sl st in next hdc.
Fasten off, leaving an 8-inch length for sewing.
Hold piece with RS facing you; working in unused lps of Row 1, join brown in first lp.
Row 3: Ch 1, hdc in same lp and in each rem lp, turn. *(7 hdc)*
Row 4: Rep Row 2.
Hold piece with RS facing you; working in rem lps of Row 3, join white in first hdc.
Row 5: Ch 1, hdc in next 5 hdc, ch 1, sl st in next hdc.
Fasten off and weave in ends.

Cherry
Hold piece with RS facing you; join red in 4th hdc of Row 5; ch 1, in same hdc work (2 hdc, ch 1, sl st).
Fasten off and weave in ends.

Finishing
With yarn needle and long ends, sew one ice cream cone to center of each strap.

Sailboat

BEGINNER

Sizes
Adult, Child

Materials
Medium (worsted) weight crochet cotton,
   small amount of blue, ecru, red and yellow
*Note: Our photographed trim was made with Lily Sugar 'n'
Cream, delft blue #28, ecru #4, red #95 and yellow #10.*
For Adult: Size G/6/4mm crochet hook (for straps and
   design) or size required for gauge
For Child: Size G/6/4mm crochet hook (for straps) or size
   required for gauge; size E/4/3.50mm crochet hook
   (for design)
Yarn needle
One pair flip-flops

Gauge
With size G hook, 6 sc = 1 inch

Instructions
*Note: For adult size, use larger hook; for child size, use larger
hook for straps and smaller hook for sailboats.*

Straps
Following General Directions on page 1 and with blue,
crochet over straps.

Sailboat (make 2)
Boat
With ecru, ch 7 loosely.
Row 1 (RS): 2 sc in 2nd ch from hook; sc in next 4 sc,
2 sc in next ch; turn. *(8 sc)*
Row 2: Ch 1, 2 sc in first sc; sc in next 6 sc, 2 sc in next sc;
turn. *(10 sc)*
Row 3: Sl st in first 5 sc, ch 7, sl st in back bump of each ch—
mast made; sl st in next 5 sc.

Fasten off, leaving an 8-inch length for sewing. Weave in
rem end.

Right Sail
Hold piece with RS facing you; join red in 2nd ch of mast;
ch 6, sc in 2nd ch from hook, hdc in next ch, dc in next ch,
tr in next ch, ch 1, sl st in last ch of mast.
Fasten off, leaving an 8-inch length for sewing. Weave in
rem end.

Left Sail
Hold piece with RS facing you; join yellow in first sl st of
mast; ch 1, sc in next sl st, hdc in next sl st, dc in next sl st,
in next sl st work (tr, ch 3, sl st).
Fasten off, leaving an 8-inch length for sewing. Weave in
rem end.

Finishing
With yarn needle and long ends, sew one sailboat to center
of each strap.

Shell

BEGINNER

Sizes
Adult, Child

Materials
Medium (worsted) weight crochet cotton,
   small amount of light blue and yellow
*Note: Our photographed trims were made with Lily Sugar 'n'
Cream, cornflower blue #83 and yellow #10.*
For Adult: Size G/6/4mm crochet hook (for straps and
   design) or size required for gauge
For Child: Size G/6/4mm crochet hook (for straps) or size
   required for gauge; size E/4/3.50mm crochet hook
   (for design)
16 (6mm) rainbow crystal pearl beads
Yarn needle
Sewing needle and matching thread
One pair flip-flops

Gauge
With size G hook, 6 sc = 1 inch

Pattern Stitches
Front Post Double Crochet (fpdc)
Yo, insert hook from front to back to front around post
(see Stitch Guide on page 24) around st indicated, draw
lp through, (yo, draw through 2 lps on hook) twice.

Back Post Double Crochet (bpdc)
Yo, insert hook from back to front to back around post
(see Stitch Guide on page 24) around st indicated, draw
lp through, (yo, draw through 2 lps on hook) twice.

Instructions
*Note: For adult size, use larger hook; for child size, use larger
hook for straps and smaller hook for shells.*

Straps
Following General Directions on page one and with light
blue, crochet over straps.

Shell (make 2)
With yellow, ch 4.

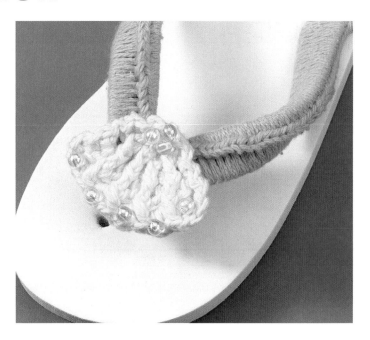

Row 1 (WS): 5 dc in 4th ch from hook (beg 3 skipped chs
count as a dc). Turn. *(6 dc)*
Row 2 (RS): Ch 3 (counts as a dc on this and following
rows), **fpdc** *(see Pattern Stitches)* around next dc, [dc in same
st (behind fpdc just made), fpdc around next dc] 3 times; dc
in 3rd ch of beg 3 skipped chs on Row 1. Turn. *(9 sts)*
Row 3: Ch 3, dc in first dc, **bpdc** *(see Pattern Stitches)* around
next st, (dc in next dc, bpdc around next st) 3 times; 2 dc in
3rd ch of turning ch-3. Turn. *(11 sts)*
Row 4: Ch 1, sc in first dc, hdc in next dc, fpdc around next
st, [in next dc work (sc, hdc, sc), fpdc around next st] 3
times; hdc in next dc, sc in 3rd ch of turning ch-3. Do not
fasten off. *(17 sts)*

Edging
Working along next side in end of rows, sk first row, in next
row work (sl st in next row, ch 1, sl st); [ch 1, sl st in next row]
twice; ch 1; working along next side, sl st in unused lp of beg
ch, ch 1; working along next side, in first row work (sl st, ch 1,
sl st); [ch 1, sl st in next row] 3 times.
Fasten off, leaving an 8-inch length for sewing. Weave in
rem end.

Finishing
Step 1: Referring to photo for placement, sew eight beads to
each shell.
Step 2: With yarn needle and long ends, sew one shell to
center of each strap.

Duck

BEGINNER

Sizes

Adult, Child

Materials

Medium (worsted) weight crochet cotton,
small amount of light green, yellow, orange and black

Note: Our photographed trim was made with Lily Sugar 'n' Cream, light green #55, yellow #10, pumpkin #132 and black #2.

For Adult: Size G/6/4mm crochet hook (for straps and design) or size required for gauge

For Child: Size G/6/4mm crochet hook (for straps) or size required for gauge; size E/4/3.50mm crochet hook (for design)

Yarn needle

One pair flip-flops

Gauge

With size G hook, 6 sc = 1 inch

Instructions

Note: For adult size, use larger hook; for child size, use larger hook for straps and smaller hook for ducks.

Straps

Following General Directions on page 1 and with light green, crochet over straps.

Duck (make 2)
Body

With yellow, ch 3 loosely.

Row 1 (RS): 2 sc in 2nd ch from hook and in next ch. Turn. *(4 sc)*

Row 2: Ch 1, 2 sc in first sc; sc in next 2 sc, 2 sc in next sc. Turn. *(6 sc)*

Row 3: Ch 1, 2 sc in first sc; sc in next 3 sc, 2 sc in next sc; sc in next sc. Turn. *(8 sc)*

Row 4: Ch 1, 2 sc in first sc; sc in next 2 sc, sc in front lp only of next 2 sc, sc in next sc, 2 sc in next sc; sc in next sc. Turn. *(10 sc)*

Row 5: Sk first sc, sl st in next 3 sc, ch 4 *(mark 2nd and 3rd chs for beak placement)*, in same sc as last sl st made work

(3 tr, 2 dc); sk next sc, sl st in next 4 sc, ch 2, hdc in same sc as last sl st made, ch 1, sl st in next sc. Do not fasten off.

Edging

Working along side of body, sc in end of each row; working along next side in unused lps of beg ch sc in each lp; working along next side, sc in end of Rows 1–4; join in first sl st of Row 5.

Fasten off, leaving an 8-inch length for sewing. Weave in rem end.

Wing

Hold piece with RS facing you; working in unused lps of Row 3, join yellow in first lp; ch 2, hdc in same lp; in next lp work (2 dc, ch 2, sl st).

Fasten off and weave in ends.

Beak

Hold piece with RS facing you; working in marked chs of Row 5, join orange in first marked ch; ch 2, sl st in 2nd ch from hook, sl st in next marked ch.

Fasten off and weave in ends.

Finishing

Step 1: Referring to photo for placement and with black, make a French Knot *(see General Directions on page 1)* for each eye.

Step 2: With yarn needle and long ends, sew one duck to center of each strap.

Pig

Sizes
Adult, Child

Materials
Medium (worsted) weight crochet cotton,
small amount of white, pink and black
Note: *Our photographed trim was made with Lily Sugar 'n' Cream, white #1, rose pink #46 and black #2.*
For Adult: Size G/6/4mm crochet hook (for straps and design) or size required for gauge
For Child: Size G/6/4mm crochet hook (for straps) or size required for gauge; size E/4/3.50mm crochet hook (for design)
Yarn needle
One pair flip-flops

Gauge
With size G hook, 6c = 1 inch

Instructions
Note: *For adult size, use larger hook; for child size, use larger hook for straps and smaller hook for pigs.*

Straps
Following General Directions on page 1 and with white, crochet over straps.

Pig (make 2)
Body
With pink, ch 6 loosely.
Row 1: 2 sc in 2nd ch from hook; sc in next 4 sc. Turn. *(6 sc)*
Row 2: Ch 1, sk first sc, sl st in next sc, sc in next 3 sc, 2 sc in next sc. Turn. *(6 sts)*
Row 3: Ch 1, 2 sc in first sc; sc in next 2 sc, 2 sc in next sc; turn, leaving rem 3 sts unworked. *(6 sc)*
Row 4: Ch 1, sc in each sc. Turn.
Row 5: Ch 1, sc in each sc. Turn. *(8 sc)*
Note: *For **sc dec**, draw up lp in 2 sts indicated, yo and draw through all 3 lps on hook.*
Row 6: Ch 3, sc in 2nd ch from hook and in next ch, sc in next 4 sc, **sc dec** *(see Note)* over next 2 sc. Turn. *(7 sc)*

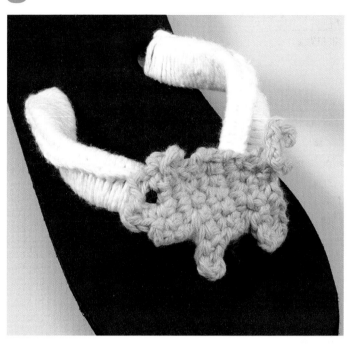

Row 7: Ch 3, sc in 2nd ch from hook and in next ch, sc in next 2 sc, 2 sc in next sc. Turn, leaving rem 4 sc unworked. *(6 sc)*
Row 8: Ch 1, sc in first 5 sc. Turn, leaving rem sc unworked. *(5 sc)*
Row 9: Ch 1, sc dec over first 2 sc; sc in next sc, ch 2, sc in 2nd ch from hook, sc in side of last sc made on Row 9, sl st in next sc, sc in last sc.
Fasten off, leaving an 8-inch length for sewing. Weave in rem end.

Ear
Join pink around 2nd sc on Row 7; ch 2, sc in 2nd ch from hook, sl st in same sc on Row 7.
Fasten off and weave in ends.

Tail
Join pink in turning ch on end of Row 1; ch 5, in 2nd ch from hook work (sl st, ch 1, sl st); in each of next 3 chs work [ch 1, sl st] twice.
Fasten off and weave in ends. Twist to shape.

Finishing
Step 1: Referring to photo for placement and with black, make a French Knot *(see General Directions on page 1)* on one side of one body and on opposite side of rem body for eyes.
Step 2: With yarn needle and long ends, sew one pig to center of each strap.

Frog

Sizes
Adult, Child

Materials
Medium (worsted) weight crochet cotton,
small amount of ecru, white, green and black
Note: Our photographed trim was made with Lily Sugar 'n Cream, ecru #4, white #1, hunter green #78 and black #2.
For Adult: Size G/6/4mm crochet hook (for straps and design) or size required for gauge
For Child: Size G/6/4mm crochet hook (for straps) or size required for gauge; size E/4/3.50mm crochet hook (for design)
Yarn needle
One pair flip-flops

Gauge
With size G hook, 6 sc = 1 inch

Pattern Stitches
Puff Stitch (puff st)
Yo, insert hook in st indicated, draw lp through, [yo, insert hook in same st, draw lp through] twice; yo and draw through all 6 lps on hook.

Front Post Half Double Crochet (fphdc)
Yo, insert hook from front to back to front around post (see Stitch Guide on page 24) of st indicated, draw lp through, yo and draw through all 3 lps on hook.

Instructions
Note: For adult size, use larger hook; for child size, use larger hook for straps and smaller hook for frogs.

Straps
Following General Directions on page 1 and with ecru, crochet over straps.

Frog (make 2)
Body
With green, ch 8.
Row 1 (WS): 2 sc in 2nd ch from hook; sc in next 5 chs, 2 sc in next ch; turn. *(9 sc)*

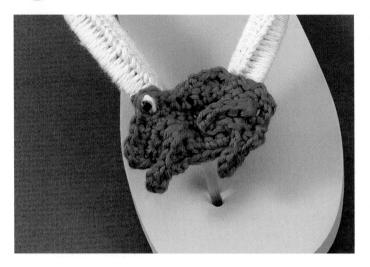

Row 2 (RS): Ch 1, 2 sc in first sc; sc in next 6 sc, 2 sc in each of next 2 sc; turn. *(12 sc)*
Mark 10th sc.
*Note: For **sc dec**, draw up lp in next 2 sc, yo and draw through all 3 lps on hook.*
Row 3: Ch 1, 2 sc in first sc; sc in next 9 sc, **sc dec** *(see Note)* over next 2 sc; turn. *(12 sc)*
Row 4: Ch 1, sc dec over first 2 sc; sc in next 10 sc; turn. *(11 sc)*
Row 5: Ch 1, 2 sc in first sc; sc in next 8 sc, sc dec; turn. *(11 sc)*
Row 6: Ch 1, sc dec over first 2 sc; sc in next 2 sc, sl st in next 3 sc, in next sc work [**puff st** *(see Pattern Stitches)*, ch 1, sl st]; sc in next sc, sl st in next sc.

Edging
Ch 1, sk next sc on Row 5, working around body in end of rows and in unused lps of beg ch, sl st in Row 6, ch 1, [sl st in next row, ch 1, sk next row] twice; ch 1, sk Row 1, sl st in first unused lp of beg ch, [ch 1, sk next ch, sl st in next ch] 3 times; ch 1, sl st in Row 1, [ch 1, sl st in next row, sl st in next row] twice; ch 1, sl st in first sc of Row 6, ch 1, sk next sc, sl st in next sc.
Fasten off, leave rem sts unworked and leaving an 8-inch length for sewing. Weave in rem end.

Front Leg
Hold piece with RS facing you and head at top; join green around post (see Stitch Guide on page 24) of 10th sc on Row 2; **fphdc** *(see Pattern Stitches)* around post of same sc; fphdc around post of next sc on Row 1; ch 3, in 2nd ch from hook work (hdc, ch 1, sl st); sc in next ch, ch 1, sl st in ch-1 sp on edging.
Fasten off and weave in ends.

Back Leg

Hold piece with RS facing you and holding Body with head towards you; join green around post of 2nd sc on Row 2, fphdc around same sc; fphdc around each of next 4 sc on Row 2; ch 1, sl st around same st as last hdc made; turn piece so bottom of body is at top; sc around each of last 3 sc just worked into, ch 4, in 2nd ch from hook work (hdc, ch 1, sl st); sc in next 2 chs, ch 1, sl st in ch-1 sp on edging.
Fasten off and weave in ends.

Finishing

Step 1: Referring to photo for placement and with white, make a Straight Stitch *(see General Directions on page 1)* on frog for each eye.
Step 2: With black, make a French Knot *(see General Directions on page 1)* in center of each eye.
Step 3: With yarn needle and long ends, sew one frog to center of each strap.

Turtle

BEGINNER

Sizes
Adult, Child

Materials
Medium (worsted) weight crochet cotton, small amount of yellow, brown, light green, green and black
Note: Our photographed trims were made with Lily Sugar 'n' Cream, yellow #10, warm brown #130, light green #55, hunter green #78 and black #2.
For Adult: Size G/6/4mm crochet hook (for straps and design) or size required for gauge
For Child: Size G/6/4mm crochet hook (for straps) or size required for gauge; size E/4/3.50mm crochet hook (for design)
Yarn needle
One pair flip-flops

Gauge
With size G hook, 6 sc = 1 inch

Pattern Stitches
Cluster (cl)
Keeping last lp of each tr on hook, 3 tr in st indicated; yo and draw through all 4 lps on hook.

Instructions
Note: For adult size, use larger hook; for child size, use larger hook for straps and smaller hook for turtles.

Straps
Following General Directions on page 1 and with yellow, crochet over straps.

Turtle (make 2)
Shell
With brown, ch 6.
Rnd 1 (RS): 2 sc in 2nd ch from hook; sc in next 3 chs, 3 sc in next ch; working on opposite side in unused lps of beg ch, sc in next 3 chs, 2 sc in next ch; join to first sc. *(13 sc)*
Rnd 2: Ch 1, 2 sc in first sc; sc in next sc, hdc in next sc, 2 hdc in next sc; hdc in next sc, sc in next sc, 3 sc in next sc; sc in next sc, hdc in next sc, 2 hdc in next sc; hdc in next sc, sc in next sc, 2 sc in next sc; join to first sc. *(19 sts)*
Rnd 3: Ch 1, 2 sc in first sc; hdc in next 8 sts, sc in next 2 sc, hdc in next 8 sts; join to first sc.
Fasten off, leaving an 8-inch length for sewing. Weave in rem end.

Head, Legs & Tail
Hold piece with RS facing you; working in front lps only, join green in first sc of Rnd 3; ch 5, sl st in 2nd ch from hook and in next 3 chs, sl st in same sc on Rnd 3—tail made; sl st in next 2 sts; * in next hdc work (sl st, ch 1, dc, ch 1, sl st in last dc made, dc, ch 1, sl st)—leg made; sl st in next 3 sts; rep from *

once more; in next sc work [sl st, ch 1, hdc, dc, **cl** *(see Pattern Stitch)*, dc, hdc, ch 1, sl st); sl st in next 3 sts, in next hdc work (sl st, ch 1, dc, ch 1, sl st in last dc made, ch 1, sl st)—leg made; sl st in next 2 sts, in next hdc work (sl st, ch 1, dc, ch 1, sl st)—leg made; sl st in next hdc; join in joining sl st.
Fasten off and weave in ends.

Trim

Hold piece with RS facing you; working around post *(see Stitch Guide on page 24)* of each st, join light green around first sc on Rnd 3 of Shell; sc around post of same st, ch 1; *sc around post of next st, ch 1; rep from * around; join in first sc.
Fasten off and weave in ends.

Finishing

Step 1: Referring to photo for placement and with black, make a French Knot *(see General Directions on page 1)* on each side of head for eyes.
Step 2: Referring to photo for placement and with yarn needle and long ends, sew one turtle to center of each strap.

Watermelon

BEGINNER

Sizes
Adult, Child

Materials
Medium (worsted) weight crochet cotton,
  small amount of white, red, light green, green and black
Note: Our photographed trims were made with Lily Sugar 'n' Cream, white #1, red #95, light green #55, hunter green #78 and black #2.
For Adult: Size G/6/4mm crochet hook (for straps and design) or size required for gauge
For Child: Size G/6/4mm crochet hook (for straps) or size required for gauge; size E/4/3.50mm crochet hook (for design)
Yarn needle
One pair flip-flops

Gauge
With size G hook, 6 sc = 1 inch

Instructions
Note: For adult size, use larger hook; for child size, use larger hook for straps and smaller hook for watermelons.

Straps
Following General Directions on page 1 and with white, crochet over straps.

Watermelon (make 2)
With red, ch 5.
Row 1 (RS): 10 tr in 5th ch from hook; ch 4, sl st in same ch as last tr made.
Fasten off, leaving an 8-inch length for sewing.
Row 2: With RS facing you and with light green make slip knot on hook and join with sc in 4th ch of beg ch-5; 2 sc in each of next 10 tr; sc in first ch of next ch-4 sp. Fasten off.
Row 3: With RS facing you, join green in back lp only of first sc; ch 1, working in back lps only, in next 20 sc work (sl st, ch 1); sl st in next sc.
Fasten off and weave in all ends.

Finishing
Step 1: Referring to photo for placement and with black, make Straight Stitches *(see General Directions on page 1)* on Row 1 of watermelon for seeds.
Step 2: With yarn needle and long ends, sew one watermelon to center of each strap.

Strawberry

BEGINNER

Sizes
Adult, Child

Materials
Medium (worsted) weight crochet cotton,
    small amount of white, red, green and black
Note: *Our photographed flip-flops were made with Lily Sugar 'n' Cream, white #1, red #95, emerald green #62 and black #2.*
For Adult: Size G/6/4mm crochet hook (for straps and
    design) or size required for gauge
For Child: Size G/6/4mm crochet hook (for straps) or size
    required for gauge; size E/4/3.50mm crochet hook (for
    design)
Yarn needle
One pair flip-flops

Gauge
With size G hook, 6 sc = 1 inch

Instructions
Note: *For adult size, use larger hook; for child size, use larger hook for straps and smaller hook for strawberrys.*

Straps
Following General Directions on page 1 and with white, crochet over straps.

Strawberry (make 2)
Berry
With red, ch 5.
Row 1 (RS): Hdc in 3rd ch from hook, sc in next ch, 2 hdc in next ch. Turn. *(5 sts)*
Row 2: Ch 2 *(counts as a hdc on this and following rows)*, hdc in first hdc and in next 3 hdc, 2 hdc in 2nd ch of beg ch-5. Turn. *(7 hdc)*
Row 3: Ch 2, hdc in first hdc and in next 5 hdc, 2 hdc in 2nd ch of turning ch-2. Turn. *(9 hdc)*
Row 4: Ch 2, sk first hdc, hdc in next hdc and in each hdc and in 2nd ch of turning ch-2. Turn. *(9 hdc)*
Row 5: Sl st in first hdc, ch 1, hdc in next 3 hdc, sl st in next

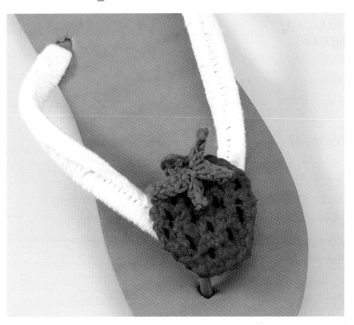

hdc, hdc in next 2 hdc, in 2nd ch of turning ch-2 work (hdc, ch 1, sl st). Do not fasten off.

Edging
Working in ends of rows and in unused lps of beg ch, work (ch 1, sl st) around piece to beg of Row 5.
Fasten off, leaving an 8-inch length for sewing. Weave in rem end.

Leaves
Hold berry with WS facing you; join green in ch-1 sp to right of center sl st of Row 5 of berry; ch 5; working in back bumps only, sl st in 3rd ch from hook, sc in next 2 chs, sl st in same ch-1 sp as joining; ch 5, sl st in 3rd ch from hook, sc in next 2 chs, sl st in center sl st of Row 5; ch 5, sl st in 3rd ch from hook, sc in next 2 chs, sl st in next ch-1 sp of Row 5; ch 5, sl st in 3rd ch from hook, sc in next 2 chs, sl st in same ch-1 sp, ch 3, sc in 2nd ch from hook and in next ch, turn (so WS of berry is facing you); sl st in same ch-1 sp as joining sl st of Row 5.
Fasten off and weave in ends.

Finishing
Step 1: Referring to photo for placement and with black, make Straight Stitches *(see General Directions on page 1)* on each strawberry for seeds.
Step 2: With yarn needle and long ends, sew one strawberry to center of each strap.

Big Bow

Sizes
Adult, Child

Materials
Novelty "fur" yarn,
   small amount of red
Note: *Our photographed trims were made with Bel Elf Eyelash, cherry red #90176 (or substitute Bernat Boa, Phoenix 381505).*
For Adult: Size G/6/4mm crochet hook (for straps and design) or size required for gauge
For Child: Size G/6/4mm crochet hook (for straps) or size required for gauge; size E/4/3.50mm crochet hook (for design)
Yarn needle
One pair flip-flops

Gauge
With size G hook, 6 sc = 1 inch

Instructions
Note: *For adult size, use larger hook; for child size, use larger hook for straps and smaller hook for bows.*

Straps
Following General Directions on page 1, crochet over straps.

Bow (make 2)
Holding 2 strands tog, ch 50. Fasten off and weave in ends.

Finishing
Slide 1 ch-50 under center 4 sts on one strap. Tie in bow. Trim ends. Rep with rem ch-50 on 2nd strap.

- -

Bow Tie

Sizes
Adult, Child

Materials
Medium (worsted) weight chenille, small amount white
Note: *Our photographed trims were made with Lion Chenille Sensations, white #100.*
For Adult: Size G/6/4mm crochet hook (for straps and design)

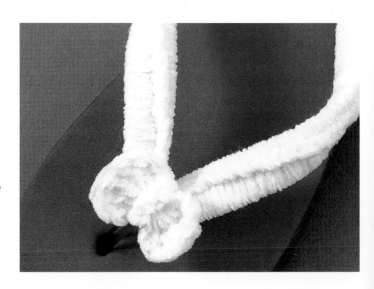

For Child: Size G/6/4mm crochet hook (for straps); size E/4/ 3.50mm crochet hook (for design)

Yarn needle

One pair flip-flops

Gauge

With size G hook, 6 sc = 1 inch

Instructions

Note: For adult size, use larger hook; for child size, use larger hook for straps and smaller hook for bow ties.

Straps

Following General Directions on page 1, crochet over straps.

Bow Tie (make 2)

Ch 4, join to form a ring.

Rnd 1: Ch 1, sc in ring, ch 1, 5 tr in ring; ch 1, in ring work (sc, sl st, sc); ch 1, 5 tr in ring; ch 1, sc in ring, sl st in joining sl st; ch 2, sl st in sl st made between sc; turn; sc in 2 chs just made, sl st in same joining sl st.

Fasten off, leaving an 8-inch length for sewing. Weave in other end.

Finishing

With yarn needle and long ends, sew one bow tie to center of each strap.

Chenille Flower

BEGINNER

Sizes

Adult, Child

Materials

Medium (worsted) weight crochet cotton,
  small amount variegated

Note: Our photographed trims were made with Caron Jewel Box, tigereye #0005.

For Adult: Size G/6/4mm crochet hook (for straps and design) or size required for gauge

For Child: Size G/6/4mm crochet hook (for straps) or size required for gauge; size E/4/3.50mm crochet hook (for design)

Yarn needle

One pair flip-flops

Gauge

With size G hook, 6 sc = 1 inch

Instructions

Note: For adult size, use larger hook; for child size, use larger hook for straps and smaller hook for flowers.

Straps

Following General Directions on page 1, crochet over straps,

keeping top of sts along inside edge of straps instead of on top of strap.

Flower (make 2)

Ch 4, join to form a ring; [ch 10, sl st in ring] 8 times.

Fasten off, leaving an 8-inch length for sewing. Weave in rem end.

Finishing

With yarn needle and long ends, sew one flower to center of each strap.

Small Tassel

BEGINNER

Sizes
Adult, Child

Materials
Fine (sport) weight yarn, small amount of peacock

Note: Our photographed trims were made with Brunswick Cotton Candy, peacock #2937.

For Adult: Size G/6/4mm crochet hook (for straps and design) or size required for gauge

For Child: Size G/6/4mm crochet hook (for straps) or size required for gauge; size E/4/3.50mm crochet hook (for design)

Yarn needle

2-inch piece of cardboard

One pair flip-flops

Gauge
With size G hook, 8 sc = 1 inch

Instructions
Note: For adult size, use larger hook; for child size, use larger hook for straps and smaller hook for loops.

Straps
Following General Directions on page 1, crochet over straps.

Tassel (make 4)
Wrap 4-feet strand of yarn around cardboard. Thread a 12-inch strand into yarn needle and insert it under strands along edge of cardboard. Tie it at top, leaving a long end to wrap around tassel. Cut strands at opposite edge of cardboard. Wrap long end around tassel about ½-inch below top and fasten securely. Trim ends.

Hanging Cord
Fold an 8-inch strand of yarn in half; insert hook through top of tassel and pull folded end through; with yarn ends, ch 4. Fasten off and weave in ends.

Finishing
Using yarn needle, sew hanging cords of two tassels to center of each strap.

Large Tassel

BEGINNER

Sizes
Adult, Child

Materials
Fine (sport) weight novelty fur yarn, small amount of variegated

Note: Our photographed trims were made with Bernat Boa, tweety bird #99823.

For Adult: Size G/6/4mm crochet hook (for straps and design) or size required for gauge

For Child: Size G/6/4mm crochet hook (for straps) or size required for gauge; size E/4/3.50mm crochet hook (for design)

Yarn needle

3-inch wide piece of cardboard

One pair flip-flops

Gauge

With size G hook, 8 sc = 1 inch

Instructions

Note: For adult size, use larger hook; for child size, use larger hook for straps and smaller hook for loops.

Straps

Following General Directions on page 1, crochet over straps.

Tassel (make 2)

Wrap 6-foot strand of yarn around cardboard. Thread a 12-inch strand into yarn needle and insert it under strands along edge of cardboard. Tie it at top, leaving a long end to wrap around tassel. Cut strands at opposite edge of cardboard. Wrap long end around tassel about ½-inch below top and fasten securely. Trim ends.

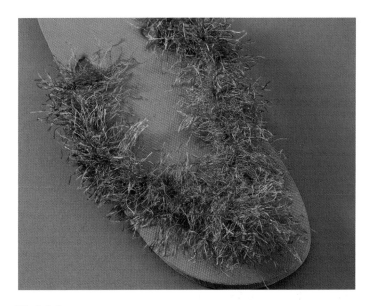

Finishing

Place top of tassels at center of straps with loose ends facing up and sew in place.

• •

Fringe

BEGINNER

Sizes

Adult, Child

Materials

Medium (worsted) weight yarn, small amount light blue
Note: Our photographed trims were made with Lion Brand Terryspun, powder blue #105

For Adult: Size G/6/4mm crochet hook (for straps and design) or size required for gauge
For Child: Size G/6/4mm crochet hook (for straps) or size required for gauge; size E/4/3.50mm crochet hook (for design)
Yarn needle
One pair flip-flops

Gauge

With size G hook, 6 sc = 1 inch

Instructions

Note: For adult size, use larger hook; for child size, use larger hook for straps and smaller hook for fringe.

Straps

Following General Directions on page 1, crochet over straps.

Fringe (make 2)

Cut 18 (4-inch) lengths. For center fringe knot, fold 1 length in half and draw folded end from right to wrong side through sc in center of 1 strap. Pull loose ends through folded section and draw knot up firmly. Tie 4 additional knots evenly spaced on each side of each center knot. Trim ends even.

A Word About Gauge

A correct stitch gauge is very important. Please take the time to work a stitch gauge swatch about 4 x 4 inches. Measure the swatch. If the number of stitches and rows are fewer than indicated under "Gauge" in the pattern, your needle is too large. Try another swatch with a smaller size hook. If the number of stitches and rows are more than indicated under "Gauge" in the pattern, your needle is too small. Try another swatch with a larger size hook.

Abbreviations & Symbols

beg .... begin/beginning
bpdc.. back post double crochet
bpsc... back post single crochet
bptr.. back post treble crochet
CC .... contrasting color
ch... chain stitch
ch-...
refers to chain or space previously made (i.e. ch-1 space)
ch sp .... chain space
cl..cluster
cm .... centimeter(s)
dc.. double crochet
dc dec..
double crochet 2 or more stitches together, as indicated
dec.................................. decrease/decreases/decreasing
dtr ....double treble crochet
fpdc...front post double crochet
fpsc .... front post single crochet
fptr .... front post treble crochet
g ....gram(s)
hdc ....half double crochet
hdc ....dechalf
double crochet 2 or more stitches together, as indicated
lp(s)...loops(s)
MC ....main color
mm.. millimeter(s)
oz.. ounce(s)
pc .... popcorn
rem ....remain/remaining
rep.. repeat(s)
rnd(s)... round(s)
RS...right side
sc... single crochet
sc dec..
single crochet 2 or more stitches together, as indicated
sk... skip
sl st...slip stitch
sp(s)..space(s)

st(s)...stitch(es)
tog... together
tr..treble crochet
trtr...triple treble
WS... wrong side
yd(s)... yard(s)
yo... yarn over

* An asterisk (or double asterisk **) is used to mark the beginning of a portion of instructions to be worked more than once; thus, "rep from * twice more" means after working the instructions once, repeat the instructions following the asterisk twice more (3 times in all).
† The dagger (or double dagger ††) identifies a portion of instructions that will be repeated again later in the same row or round.
[ ] Brackets are used to enclose instructions that should be worked the exact number of times specified immediately following the brackets, such as "[2 sc in next dc, sc in next dc] twice." They are also used to set off and clarify a group of stitches that are to be worked all into the same space or stitch, such as "in next corner sp work [2 dc, ch 1, 2 dc]."
[ ] Brackets and () parentheses are used to provide additional information to clarify instructions.
Join—join with a sl st unless otherwise specified.

The patterns in this book are written using United States terminology. Terms that have different English equivalents are noted below.

United States	English
single crochet (sc)	double crochet (dc)
double crochet (dc)	treble (tr)
treble crochet (tr)	double treble (dtr)
skip (sk)	miss
slip stitch (sl st)	slip stitch (ss) or single crochet
gauge	tension
yarn over (YO)	yarn over hook (YOH)

Metric Chart

INCHES INTO MILLIMETERS & CENTIMETERS (Rounded off slightly)

inches	mm	cm	inches	cm	inches	cm	inches	cm
1/8	3		5	12.5	21	53.5	38	96.5
1/4	6		5 1/2	14	22	56	39	99
3/8	10	1	6	15	23	58.5	40	101.5
1/2	13	1.3	7	18	24	61	41	104
5/8	15	1.5	8	20.5	25	63.5	42	106.5
3/4	20	2	9	23	26	66	43	109
7/8	22	2.2	10	25.5	27	68.5	44	112
1	25	2.5	11	28	28	71	45	114.5
1 1/4	32	3.2	12	30.5	29	73.5	46	117
1 1/2	38	3.8	13	33	30	76	47	119.5
1 3/4	45	4.5	14	35.5	31	79	48	122
2	50	5	15	38	32	81.5	49	124.5
2 1/2	65	6.5	16	40.5	33	84	50	127
3	75	7.5	17	43	34	86.5		
3 1/2	90	9	18	46	35	89		
4	100	10	19	48.5	36	91.5		
4 1/2	115	11.5	20	51	37	94		

CROCHET HOOKS METRIC CONVERSION CHART

U.S.	1/B	2/C	3/D	4/E	5/F	6/G	8/H	9/I	10/J	10½/K	N
Continental-mm	2.25	2.75	3.25	3.5	3.75	4.25	5	5.5	6	6.5	9.0

Standard Yarn Weight System

Categories of yarn, gauge ranges and recommended hook sizes

Yarn Weight Symbol & Category Names	1 SUPER FINE	2 FINE	3 LIGHT	4 MEDIUM	5 BULKY	6 SUPER BULKY
Type of Yarns in Category	Sock, Fingering, Baby	Sport, Baby	DK, Light Worsted	Worsted, Afghan, Aran	Chunky, Craft, Rug	Bulky, Roving
Crochet Gauge* Ranges in Single Crochet to 4 inch	21–32 sts	16–20 sts	12–17 sts	11–14 sts	8–11 sts	5–9 sts
Recommended Hook in Metric Size Range	2.25–3.5 mm	3.5–4.5 mm	4.5–5.5 mm	5.5–6.5 mm	6.5–9 mm	9 mm and larger
Recommended Hook U.S. Size Range	B1–E4	E4–7	7–I9	I-9–K-10½	K-10½–M-13	M-13 and larger

* GUIDELINES ONLY: The above reflect the most commonly used gauges and hook sizes for specific yarn categories.

Crochet Stitch Guide

Chain - ch:
YO, draw through lp on hook.

Single Crochet - sc:
Insert hook in st, YO and draw through, YO and draw through both lps on hook.

Reverse Single Crochet -
Reverse sc:
Work from left to right, insert hook in sp or st indicated (**a**), draw lp through sp or st - 2 lps on hook (**b**); YO and draw through lps on hook.

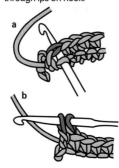

Half Double Crochet - hdc:
YO, insert hook in st, YO, draw through, YO and draw through all 3 lps on hook.

Double Crochet - dc:
YO, insert hook in st, YO, draw through, (YO and draw through 2 lps on hook) twice.

Triple Crochet - trc:
YO twice, insert hook in st, YO, draw through, (YO and draw through 2 lps on hook) 3 times.

Slip Stitch - sl st:
(a) Used for Joinings
Insert hook in indicated st, YO and draw through st and lp on hook.

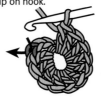

(b) Used for Moving Yarn Over
Insert hook in st, YO draw through st and lp on hook.

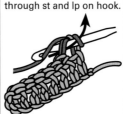

Front Loop - FL:
The front loop is the loop toward you at the top of the stitch.

Back Loop - BL:
The back loop is the loop away from you at the top of the stitch.

Post:
The post is the vertical part of the stitch.

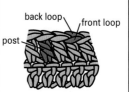

back loop   front loop
post

Overcast Stitch is worked loosely to join crochet pieces.

American School of Needlework ®
excellence in instruction

DRG Publishing
306 East Parr Road
Berne, IN 46711
©2005 American School of Needlework Inc.
TOLL-FREE ORDER LINE or to request a free catalog (800) 582-6643
Customer Service (800) 282-6643, Fax (800) 882-6643

Visit AnniesAttic.com.

Customer Service (800**) 282-6643, fax (**800**) 882-6643**

We have made every effort to ensure the accuracy and completeness of these instructions. We cannot, however, be responsible for human error, typographical mistakes or variations in individual work.